NUBIAN KINGDOM (1000 BC):

CULTURE, CONFLICTS AND ITS GLITTERING TREASURES

ANCIENT HISTORY BOOK 5TH GRADE | CHILDREN'S ANCIENT HISTORY

BABY PROFESSOR

First Edition, 2019

Published in the United States by Speedy Publishing LLC, 40 E Main Street, Newark, Delaware 19711 USA.

© 2019 Baby Professor Books, an imprint of Speedy Publishing LLC

All rights reserved.

Without limiting the rights under the copyright reserved above, no part of this publication may be reproduced, stored in or introduced into a retrieval system, or transmitted, in any form, or by any means (electronic, mechanical, photocopying, recording, or otherwise), without the prior written permission of the copyright owner.

All images in this book have been reproduced with the knowledge and prior consent of the artists concerned, and no responsibility is accepted by producer, publisher, or printer for any infringement of copyright or otherwise arising from the contents of this publication.

Baby Professor Books are available at special discounts when purchased in bulk for industrial and sales-promotional use. For details contact our Special Sales Team at Speedy Publishing LLC, 40 E Main Street, Newark, Delaware 19711 USA. Telephone (888) 248-4521 Fax: (210) 519-4043. www.speedybookstore.com

10 9 8 7 6 * 5 4 3 2 1

Print Edition: 9781541950399

Digital Edition: 9781541952195

See the world in pictures. Build your knowledge in style.

https://www.speedypublishing.com/

Table of Contents

Often, when people think about ancient African civilizations, ancient Egypt, with its towering Pyramids and mysterious Sphinx, attracts the most attention. Africa, however, is a continent rich in history with many unique and fascinating cultures. A neighbor to ancient Egypt was Nubia, a powerful kingdom that existed for thousands of years. Let's learn about this interesting and wealthy African civilization and its connections to ancient Egypt.

Where Was Nubia?

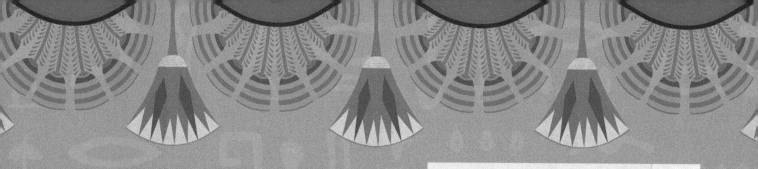

The ancient kingdom of Nubia was located in the northeastern region of Africa where the present-day countries of Egypt and Sudan are located.

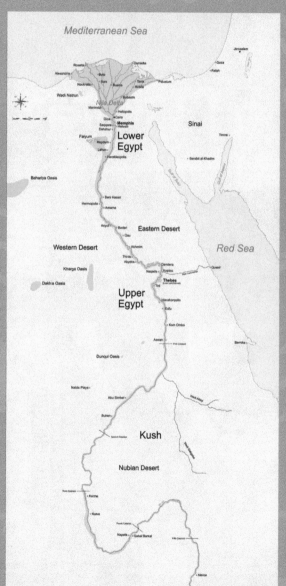

Ancient Egypt Map

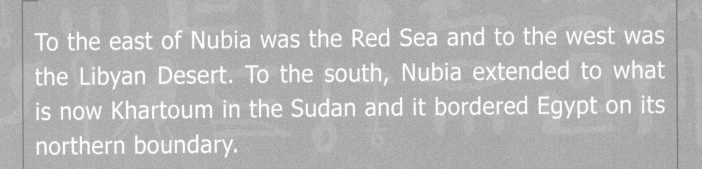

To the east of Nubia was the Red Sea and to the west was the Libyan Desert. To the south, Nubia extended to what is now Khartoum in the Sudan and it bordered Egypt on its northern boundary.

Khartoum, Sudan

The Nile River flowed through Nubia on its way to the Mediterranean Sea. Although the region was arid, the flood waters from the Nile left deposits of fertile soil on the land so farmers could cultivate their crops.

Nile River

The Cataracts of the Nile

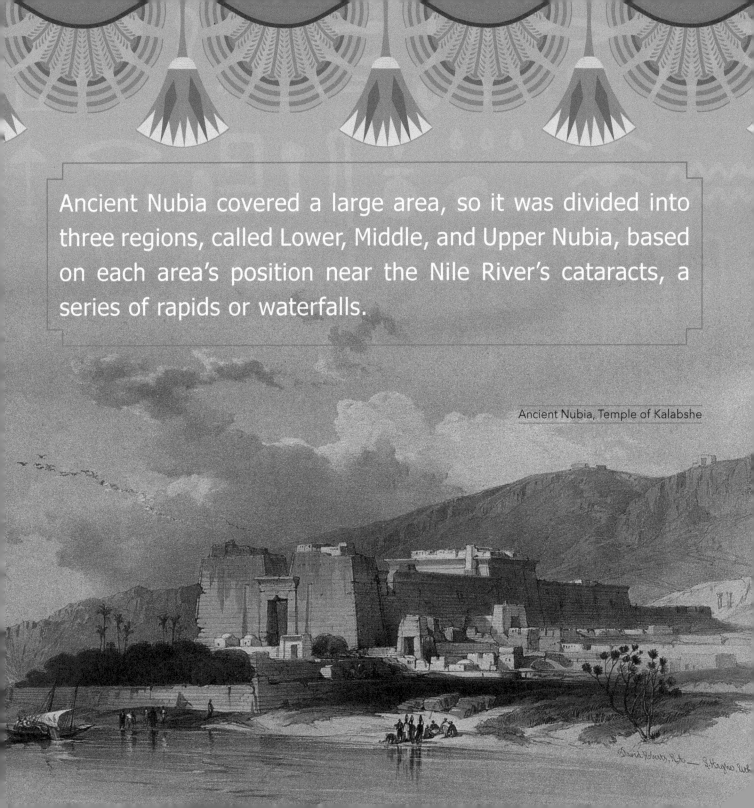

Ancient Nubia covered a large area, so it was divided into three regions, called Lower, Middle, and Upper Nubia, based on each area's position near the Nile River's cataracts, a series of rapids or waterfalls.

Ancient Nubia, Temple of Kalabshe

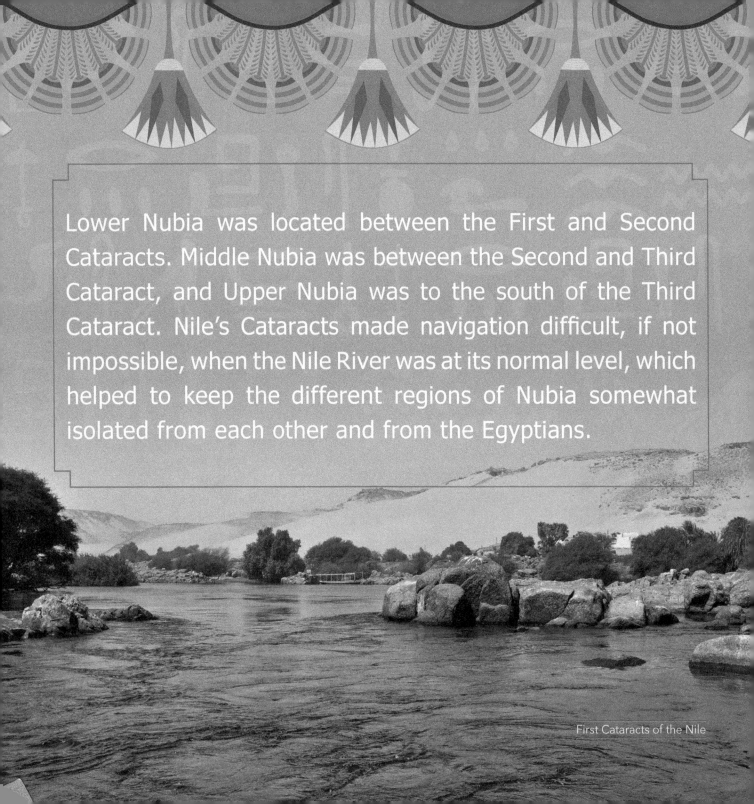

Lower Nubia was located between the First and Second Cataracts. Middle Nubia was between the Second and Third Cataract, and Upper Nubia was to the south of the Third Cataract. Nile's Cataracts made navigation difficult, if not impossible, when the Nile River was at its normal level, which helped to keep the different regions of Nubia somewhat isolated from each other and from the Egyptians.

First Cataracts of the Nile

Second Cataracts of the Nile

Third Cataracts of the Nile

Nubia in Pre-History

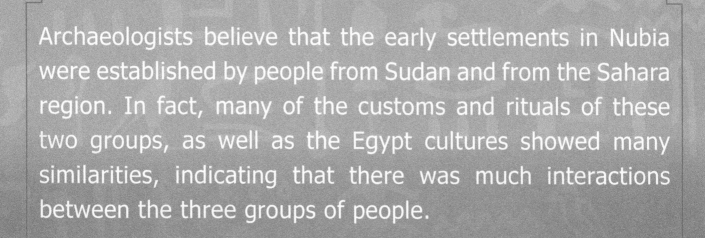

Archaeologists believe that the early settlements in Nubia were established by people from Sudan and from the Sahara region. In fact, many of the customs and rituals of these two groups, as well as the Egypt cultures showed many similarities, indicating that there was much interactions between the three groups of people.

Nubia, Temple of Amun in Naqa

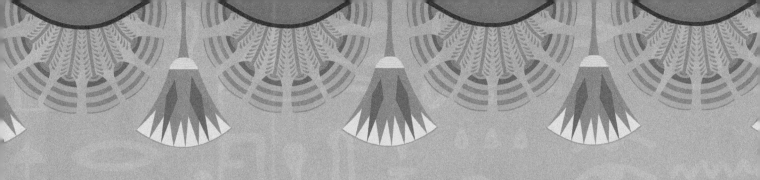

Man and Woman Harvesting

Around 5000 BC, the settlements grew larger and the people moved from small hunter-gatherer societies to farmers and livestock tenders. They developed a tiered government with different levels of authority.

Nabta Playa and the Ancient
Astronomers of the Nubian Desert

The Nubians even built devices to record astronomical measurements nearly 2,000 years before Druids built Stonehenge in England.

Trade Routes With Egypt

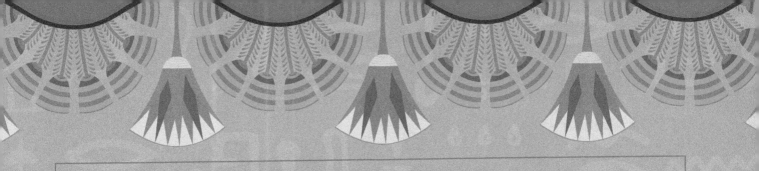

Numerous Egyptian artifacts have been unearthed in Nubia to demonstrate that there was a vigorous trade between the two adjacent cultures. These included copper pots, gold objects, tools, beads, and jewelry.

Copper Pot

Ancient Gold Bowl

Mirror

Ancient Eyptian Jewelry Beads

Gold Ram Head Amulet

Nubia was home to gold, iron, and precious gemstone mines, which provided the Nubian people with valuable resources to trade with its neighbors.

Additionally, the Egyptians imported ivory, incense, ebony, gold, and more from central Africa via trade routes that traveled through Nubia. Eventually, the Egyptians decided that if they seized the Nubian land, they could control the valuable resources.

Ivory plaque from Nimrud depicting two Egyptians. From the British Museum

Egyptian Incense Burner

Gold "Aegis" with the head of Sakhmet

This led to years of intermittent conflict between the Nubians and the Egyptians.

The Egyptians in Nubia

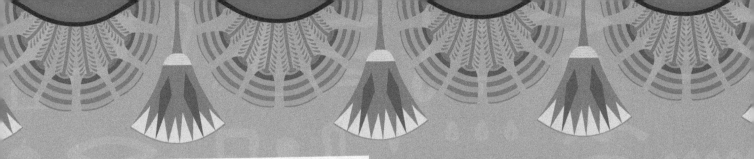

Mirgissa, one of the largest
fortresses in Nubia

Between 2040 and 1640 BC, Egypt started moving in on Nubia, taking control of the trade routes and gold mines. They build a series of forts along the Nile River to ensure the safe passage of trade goods going into Egypt.

Massive Fortress Buhen In Ancient Capital Of Egyptian Nubia

Nubians mix with the ancient Egyptians

The Nubians became more and more integrated into Egyptian culture. Marriages and political partnerships formed between the people of Nubia and the people of Egypt.

A scene of Nubian king in the 25th dynasty

They shared a common language and religious beliefs. Nubian warriors joined the Egyptian military. The Egyptians were close to completely annexing the Nubian empire.

Egyptian soldiers

The Nubian Kingdom of Kush

One particular region in Nubia, called Kush, or Cush, grew very powerful around the year 1000 BC. The center of this kingdom was the prosperous city of Meroe, the region's capital.

Ruins of Naqa Meroe, in ancient Kush, Sudan, Africa

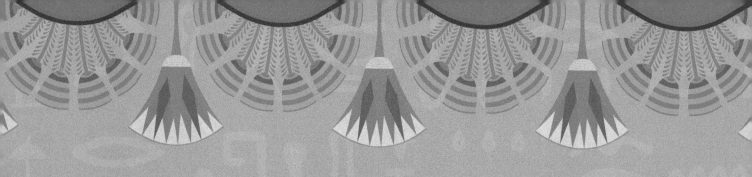

The city was the site of grand architecture, stunning art, and noble kings and queens. The Kushite city thrived for hundreds of years and was a robust trading post with a healthy economy.

Relief of a ruler, a Candace of Meroë named Kandake Amanitore

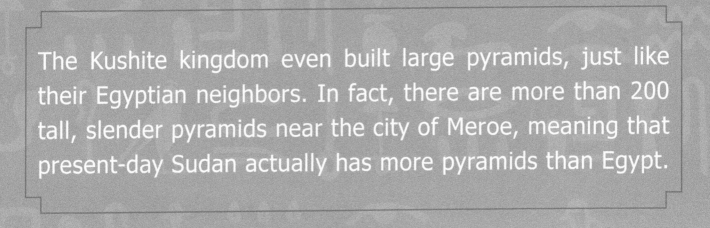

The Kushite kingdom even built large pyramids, just like their Egyptian neighbors. In fact, there are more than 200 tall, slender pyramids near the city of Meroe, meaning that present-day Sudan actually has more pyramids than Egypt.

Sudan Meroe Pyramids

A Wealthy and Independent Kingdom

Pyramids in Sudan, built by the rulers of the kingdom of Kush

The kingdom of Kush was rather isolated from Egypt and surrounding areas, thanks to the sands of the Sahara Desert and the rapids of the Nile River. This isolation allowed Kush to grow strong and powerful without interference up until the fourth century AD.

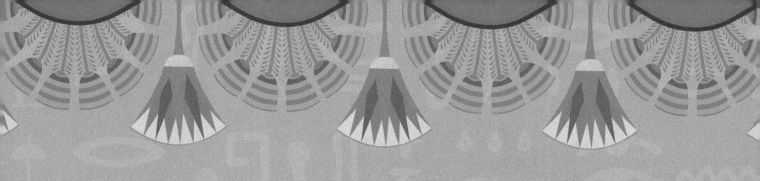

The Kushites took advantage of the many gold mines in their country to became expert gold workers, created beautiful golden artwork.

Kushite necklace spacer

The Kushite army also grew stronger. At the same time, the Egyptians were weakened by repeated attacks from three different enemies—the Persians, the Greeks, and the Assyrians. This left the Egyptians vulnerable to invasion.

Kushites

Kush Rules Over Egypt

The Egyptians were so distracted holding off attacks from the Greeks, Assyrians, and Persians and dealing with internal strife, that the Kushites were not on their radar. Following Pharaoh Ramses II's reign, the government and economy in Egypt experienced a sharp decline.

Pharaoh Ramses II

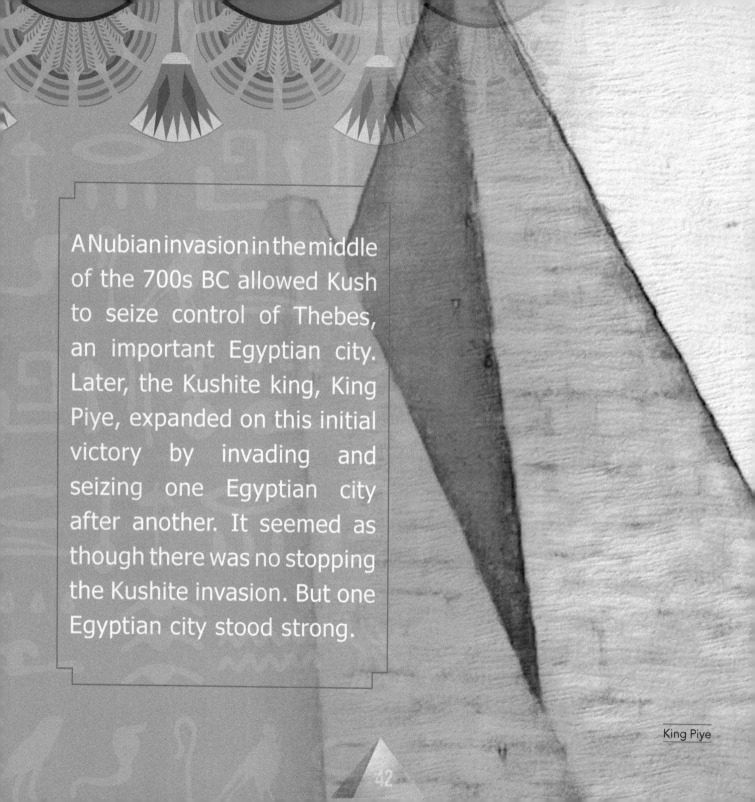

A Nubian invasion in the middle of the 700s BC allowed Kush to seize control of Thebes, an important Egyptian city. Later, the Kushite king, King Piye, expanded on this initial victory by invading and seizing one Egyptian city after another. It seemed as though there was no stopping the Kushite invasion. But one Egyptian city stood strong.

King Piye

The Battle For Hermopolis

The invasions of the other Egyptian cities met with little resistance so the Kushite king, Piye, believed that his army would have an easy time seizing control of the city of Hermopolis.

Hermopolis

The citizens of Hermopolis, however, refused to surrender to the Nubian forces. King Piye told his men, "Surround the city and capture its people. Let not the peasants go forth to the field and let not the plowman plow." Still, the people of Hermopolis stood strong.

Hermopolis

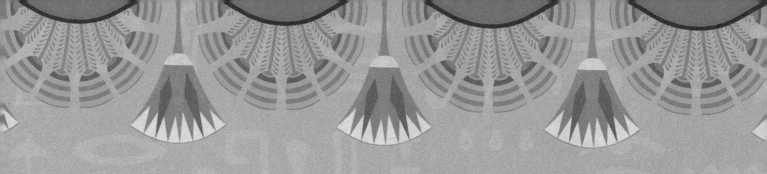

The battle rages for five months. The people of Hermopolis ran out of food and supplies and its citizens were dying of starvation. The entire city was filled with the stench of corpses rotting in the desert heat. Finally, Hermopolis surrendered to the Kushites. After the fall of Hermopolis, King Piye announced that he was the new pharaoh of both Kush and Egypt.

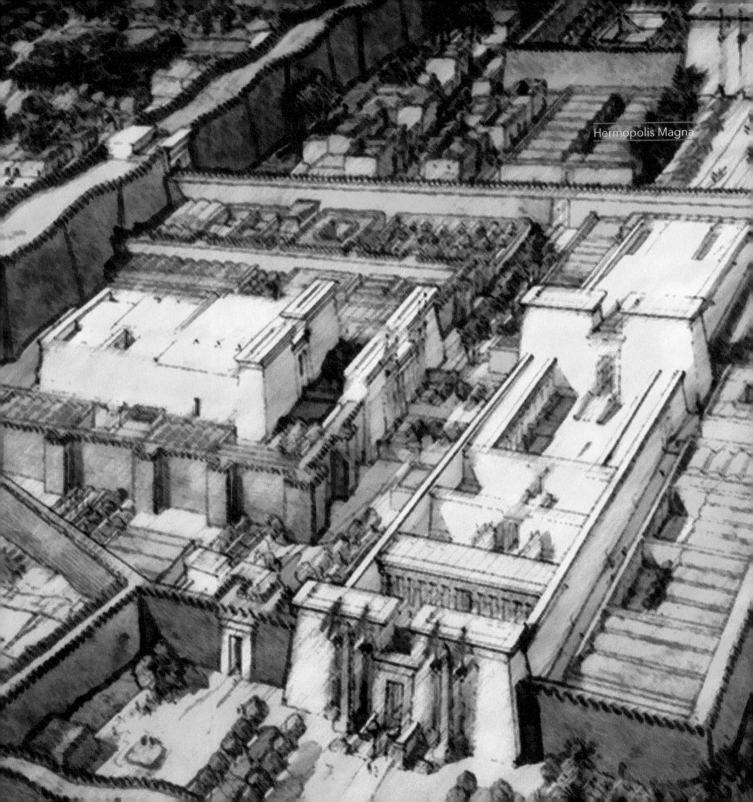

Hermopolis Magna

Nubian Control of Egypt

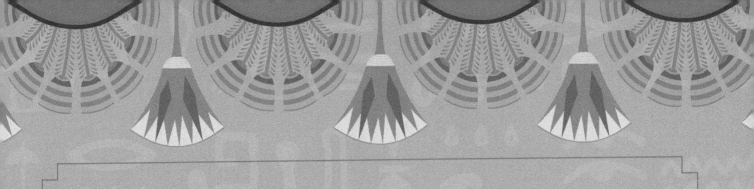

The Kushites from Nubia ruled over Egypt for nearly one hundred years. During their reign, the Nubians left their mark on Egyptian culture. Enormous temples were constructed to honor both Nubian and Egyptian gods. Rich treasures were buried in tombs around the desert.

Ruins of Amun temple Naqa Meroe, ancient Kush, Sudan

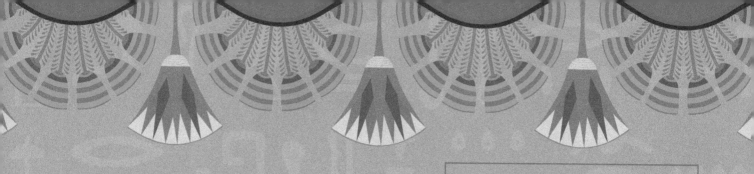

Kushite Kingdom

More importantly, the Nubian rulers stimulated more trade between the various cultures around the Red and Mediterranean Seas, as well as the interior of Africa. Under the control of the Nubians, the Egyptian economy rebounded. The Nubian rule over Egypt was short-lived, in part because of the Kushite kings' hunger for more.

The Ousting of the Nubians

The Nubians from Kush may have maintained control over Egypt for a lot longer if they hadn't grown power hungry. Instead of concentrating on ruling Egypt and the lands in their holdings, the Kushite rulers wanted to expand the empire and seize more territories. They engaged the Assyrians in a war. The Assyrians, however, were more powerful than the Nubians thought. In fact, the Assyrians warriors were coming off a victory in their conquest of the Fertile Crescent region. When the Assyrians invaded Egypt in 663 BC, the Nubians were overwhelmed. They retreated from Egypt back to Kush in Nubia.

Assyrian War Chariot

Back In Their Own Land

Ancient temple in Meroe, Sudan

After they were ousted from Egypt, the Kushites were down, but not defeated. They simply retreated back into Nubia and continued ruling over their own land. For the next one thousand years, the Nubia empire grew and thrived, taking advantage of the gold and iron ore deposits in the region.

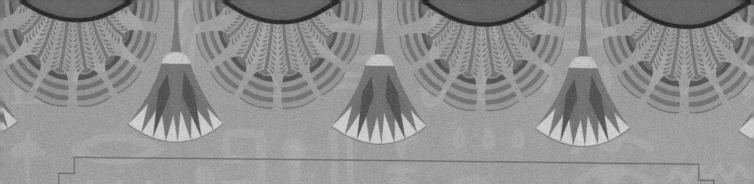

The Nubians developed Africa's first ironworking center and even helped spread knowledge of ironworking to other parts of the continent. In part because of this, the Nubian culture was an important center of commerce and trade for hundreds of years.

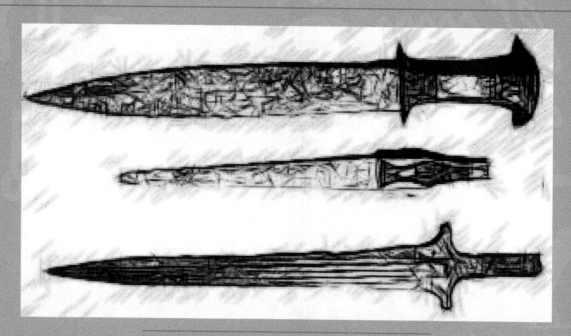

Ancient Nubian iron and bronze short swords (daggers)

The Fall of the Nubian Empire

Around 350 AD, the Nubian kingdom of Kush fell to invaders from the kingdom of Aksum. In the fourth and fifth centuries AD, the Roman Empire expanded into Nubia. Attempts were made to convert the Nubians to Christianity. In fact, when the capital city of Meroe collapsed, a new Christian kingdom took its place, called Makuria.

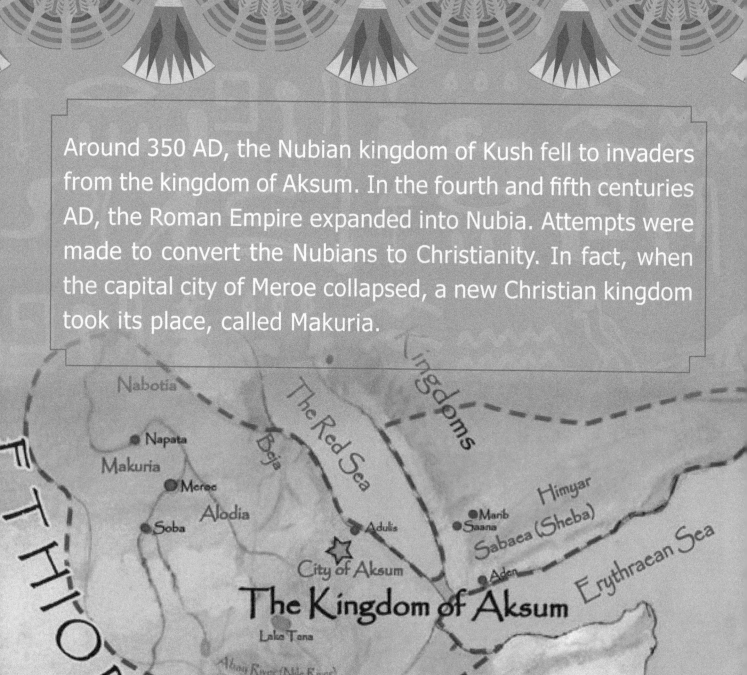

Nabotia

Napata

Beja

Kingdoms

The Red Sea

Makuria

Meroe

Alodia

Himyar

Soba

Marib
Saana

Sabaea (Sheba)

Adulis

ETHIOPIA

City of Aksum

Aden

Erythraean Sea

The Kingdom of Aksum

Lake Tana

Abay River (Nile River)

ABYSSINIA

PUNT

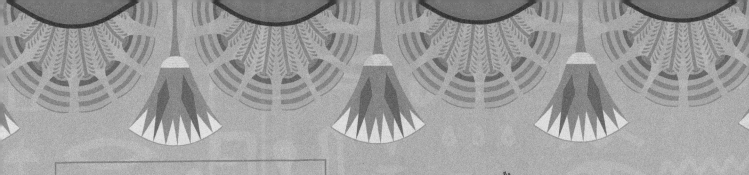

With it came new, large-scale construction projects to build massive cathedrals and monasteries. The religion wasn't the only thing to change for the people of Nubia. The Christians also brought in new languages, societal structures, and laws. The traditions and customs that made Nubia a unique ancient culture were changing and evolving.

Aksum Churches

Nubia Today

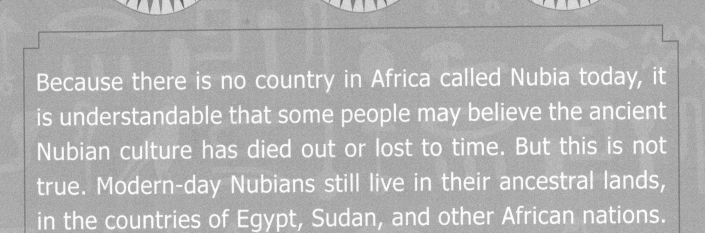

Because there is no country in Africa called Nubia today, it is understandable that some people may believe the ancient Nubian culture has died out or lost to time. But this is not true. Modern-day Nubians still live in their ancestral lands, in the countries of Egypt, Sudan, and other African nations.

Shepherds at the deserts of Sudan

Today's Nubians have been vocal about developments that infringe upon their ancient lands. In 1970, the Aswan High Dam on the Nile River flooded some of the Nubian's ancestral homelands and destroying significant archaeological sites.

Aswan High Dam

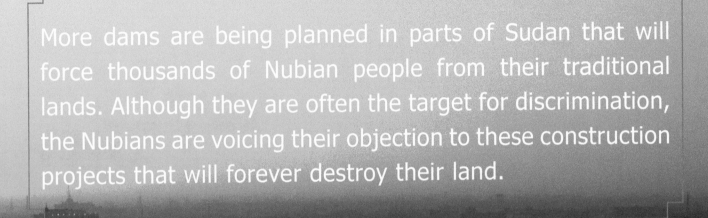

More dams are being planned in parts of Sudan that will force thousands of Nubian people from their traditional lands. Although they are often the target for discrimination, the Nubians are voicing their objection to these construction projects that will forever destroy their land.

A sunset view of river Nile in Khartoum, Sudan

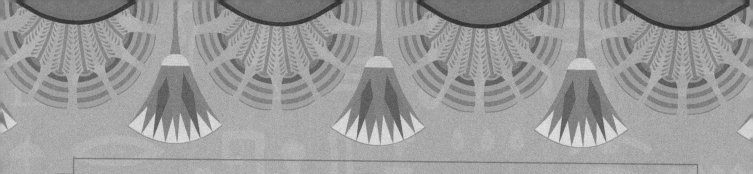

Summary

The ancient Nubian culture was rich and powerful, rivaling that of the ancient Egyptians. For thousands of years, the Nubian people built prosperous cities and fierce armies from the wealth they gained from the gold, iron ore, and precious gemstone mines that were common in their lands just south of present-day Egypt.

Now that you know about ancient Nubia, you are ready to learn about the other complex, sophisticated, artistic, and powerful cultures of ancient Africa.

Old ruins of Naga city in Sudan

The ancient pyramids of Meroe in Sudan's desert

Visit

BABY PROFESSOR
EDUCATION KIDS

www.BabyProfessorBooks.com

to download Free Baby Professor eBooks and view
our catalog of new and exciting Children's Books

9 781541 950399